AF477643

Autumn at the Lake and Other Poems

BY

Orville Lindsey Scott

FOR THE *Glory* OF GOD

DAVID CLANTON

PREFACE

My mother loved poetry and kept scrapbooks of poems from newspapers and magazines.

Growing up I began memorizing poems, especially Longfellow, Burns and Kipling but I did not continue this as a teen-ager. I was too busy playing baseball and working on my family's dairy farm.

As a journalist for the Baptist General Convention of Texas I was encouraged to write theme poems for Evangelism Conferences and other events.

Writing poems is not always easy for me, but sometimes the words seem to flow. I was driving on LBJ Freeway in Dallas on the way to a wedding shower when I dictated the "I Do" poem to my wife.

Some of the poems are in response to pastors and Sunday School teachers who want to use them to make their own greeting cards or to include in their sermons.

God Speaks

Across the pages of time

In divine prose and rhyme,

God speaks to our hearts

Through His Spirit sublime.

ORVILLE SCOTT

ORVILLE SCOTT . . .

*"His love for Christ has affected positively every aspect of his life,
including family, profession, friendships, and poetry.
He wants everyone to know Jesus as Savior and Lord..."*

Orville Scott's poems are a treasure in and of themselves, but they become even more meaningful when placed in the context of the life of the poet and the settings or occasions for the poems. One does not have to know the poet, of course, to enjoy and appreciate the poems in this book, but I believe to know something about Orville Scott will add another dimension of enjoyment for those who read this special collection of his poetry.

First and foremost, he is a deeply dedicated disciple of the Lord Jesus Christ. His love for Christ has affected positively every aspect of his life, including family, profession, friendships, and poetry. He wants everyone to know Jesus as Savior and Lord and is a persistent evangelist, sharing the way of salvation in both spoken and written words. He utilizes his poetry to personally share his faith, such as *"A Smile."* The poems in this book, like *"Keep Looking Unto Jesus"* and *"Whatever It Takes,"* are only samples of Orville's many poetic creations centered in Christ.

Second only to his love for Christ is his love for his family. He adores and appreciates Emma Jean, his wife, and frequently expresses his devotion to her in poetry, as evidenced by several of the poems in this book. He also cares deeply for his three children, James, Elizabeth, and John, and their families including his grandchildren, Travis, Rebekah, Rachel, Michael, and Emily. Enjoy the poems dedicated to them.

His relationship with Jesus Christ has led him to be very involved in church life. He has served in many capacities including deacon, Sunday School teacher, and committee member. With his servant heart he contributes to the fellowship of the churches where he has been a member. The first contact many people had with the First Baptist Church of Richardson was being greeted by Orville Scott on the parking lot in his role as parking assistant. After moving to East Texas he became a Sunday School teacher at the First Baptist Church of Canton. Because of his church commitment he is aware of the challenges faced by the pastor and the pastor's wife and he loves and supports them, as evidenced in the poem *"To the Pastor's Wife."*

Orville enjoys life—friends, special events, good food, and holidays—as indicated in his poems featuring Thanksgiving, Christmas, Valentines, anniversaries, birthdays, and *"A Good Place to Eat."* His thoughtfulness is demonstrated in the many poems that he has sent to persons at special times in their lives, such as births, deaths, retirements, promotions, all simply signed O. Scott. He has roved the world, as indicated in

"*Touching Latvia,*" but Dallas was his home for decades and he cared for the city and celebrated its special features, such as "*Thanksgiving Square,*" and its personalities, such as Norvell Slater, who for over forty years hosted the Hymns We Love program over Dallas radio.

He often expressed his appreciation for God's creation through poems about nature and animals. Born in East Texas, he grew up on a dairy farm, and after retiring moved back to East Texas, a place he described with affection in "*Ode to East Texas.*" His interest in animals is seen in the humorous "On Seeing My First Emu" and the prose parable "*The Little Maverick.*" He painted poetic pictures of nature such as "*A Flower,*" "*Autumn at the Lake,*" "*Standing in the Wind,*" "*The Hickory,*" and "*Snow 2011.*"

Orville's career was as a skilled professional journalist. He graduated with a degree in journalism from the University of Texas at Austin. After working for the Austin American-Statesman and editing two trade journals he began work in 1959 with the Baptist General Convention of Texas in the office of public relations. He left the BGCT in 1965 to be editor of Charity and Children in North Carolina for three years and then after two years of post-graduate study at the University of Missouri he returned to the BGCT in 1970 to be the Texas Baptist press representative. He remained with the BGCT as coordinator of news and information services until his retirement in 1996. Throughout the years he wrote thousands of news and feature stories. After retirement he continues to write, both prose and poetry, and enjoys his country home, family, friends, and church.

Orville's quiet, unassuming manner cloaks a fierce devotion to excellence in his craft and a dogged persistence in developing a story. This combination of genuine humility and professional excellence has brought him acclaim from his fellow journalists. He was elected president of the Dallas chapter of the Religious Public Relations Council (now the Religion Communicators Council) and of the Texas Baptist Communications Association and received a number of national awards for news and feature writing.

Outstanding qualities of Orville's life, such as compassion, warmth, and sincerity, have attracted a host of appreciative friends. He wrote in poetic terms that of all the works of the Master's art "*the greatest to me is a caring heart.*" Orville is indeed an example of the Master's art.

Colleagues who have worked closely with him have expressed appreciation for his loyalty, integrity, and thoughtfulness. Upon Scott's retirement Tom Brannon, who had been his "boss" for 16 years as the BGCT communications director, said of him: "*His unswerving loyalty, his commitment to the Lord's work, and his sweet spirit have been humbling, gratifying, and inspiring to me.*" An army of persons who know Orville Scott echo that sentiment. And this collection of poems provides an added insight into why that is true.

BILL PINSON

Autumn at the Lake

In the soothing calm of early morn,
I worship "beside the still waters"
Mid a celebration of beauty,
A symphony of love from on high.

Surrounded by tranquil woods,
The lake shimmers like a jewel,
The quiet is broken only by a bass'
Silver splash, spreading widening circles.

A breeze stirs miniature wavelets
That sparkle like myriad diamonds,
Soothing my worn and weary spirit,
Drawing my soul closer to God.

Frocked in fall hues along the shore,
Oak and cypress stretch colorful limbs
In joyous thanksgiving to the lake
And azure sky that touches eternity.

Beneath the lake's mirror surface
Schools of fish scurry quickly away,
Pausing to gaze at the intruder
Who dares to share their paradise.

Just above the water, three turtles
Bask on a snag in the golden sun.
Far up the lake, a long-legged crane
Looks for breakfast at the water's edge.

I hate to leave the joys of fall,
But all too soon my duties call…
Yes, I'll meet God beside the lake
Tomorrow morn when I awake.

A Psalm of Thanksgiving

Thank you Lord for the gift of life

And for your peace amid the strife;

For joyous freshness of the spring

With every green and growing thing.

For summer sun and gentle rain

And for the autumn's golden grain,

Oh Lord, we lift our voice in praise

And pray to serve you all our days!

O&S

STANDING IN THE *Wind*

Outside my window
Bare limbs leap and soar
In a captive dance
With the north wind's roar.

How soon summer's gone,
Winter comes so fast,
But the hopes of youth
Soar above the blast!

Like trees we must meet
Whatever life sends,
But we have a Savior
Who leads past the winds.

When icy storms beat
Upon life's window pane,
The Lord stands beside us
Guiding through the rain.

The Hickory

No mortal knows how long it stood,
Crowning the sky above the wood,
A lofty home for feathered fowl
From tiny wren to big-eyed owl.

From squirrel's cache at first it grew
Nourished by sun and morning dew,
Sleeping through winter's icy pall,
Hailing spring in a new green shawl.

Hardened by drought, fire and gale,
It met each test on nature's scale
Until at last it stood forth tall,
Reigning supremely over all.

In its shade stood a man one day,
Tried in soul on the pilgrim's way.
Heaven's winds, in soft refrain,
Said, "Come up to the higher plain."

He longed to sweep to realms on high
In verdant arms that brush the sky;
As forest chorus sang its best,
His heart grew calm within his breast.

With newfound joy he built a home
In easy view of the lofty dome,
His limbs were strong, his spirit free,
A brother to the mighty tree.

In life's sweet prime he brought his son
To share the best that nature's done.
As tender youth and hardy teen
The boy, too, loved the changing scene.

In early spring with gleeful shout
He ran to meet each new green sprout.
That sheltered him from summer heat
And shared in fall a sweet nutmeat.

From tireless limbs his spirit flew
Beyond the arch that spanned the blue,
Until at last he came no more,
Leaving the friends as they were before.

One flowering spring the son comes home,
Seeking there what he left to roam,
But passing time must take its toll
On all of life except the soul!

His father's limbs are withered now,
And snows of winter crown his brow,
For life's great race is almost run,
And soon he'll greet the Risen Son.

The mighty tree still stands nearby,
But bare dead arms embrace the sky,
And a sad young man wonders why
With gift of life we all must die.

Let who for wealth and fame hath yearned
Heed the lesson from the hick'ry learned:
Happy are they who meet the call
To be a friend to one and all.

In life the great tree gave its best,
And after death, the earth it blest. . .
Now in the glade a sapling grows,
Nourished by sun and winter snows.

I DO

There's power divine in the words "I Do,"

For all that I am, I pledge to you.

And whither thou goest, there I will go,

From dewy dawn through sunset's glow!

Hand in hand we'll stride through life,

Embracing together each joy and strife,

And if appointed to go before,

I'll wait for you at Heaven's door!

QoS

Faith

O'er stormy seas

I've seen you sail

With brightest smile

Thru fiercest gale.

So all can see

What lives within

Is faith serene

That's bound to win!

OϼS

TRUE
Success

o you measure a person's life

By his degree of wealth and fame,

Or how he stood in toil and strife,

And what he did in Jesus' name?

Fame will fade at the close of day

And worldly treasures rust away,

But we can take thru Heaven's door

The love we give on the earthly shore!

QℓS

THE BEGGAR

I gave a beggar a loaf of bread
And heard him say with bowed head,
"What kind of God made me this way?
Please tell me there's a better day!"
But I had much to do that day
And soon forgot as I rushed away.

He came again 'ere the day had flown
And touched me with his wretched moan,
I asked the Lord, "What must I do?"
He said, "That wretch is my son, too;
Tell of the miracle he's never seen;
My blood can make the foulest clean!"

I met him again on a Sunday morn,
And he had the look of a man reborn.
I thought again of his mournful cry,
But he smiled at me with head held high
And said as he looked me in the eye,
"I'll see you in Heaven by and by!"

THE *Caring Heart*

Some are given a golden voice

That helps them be the people's choice,

And some can write with glowing pen

To move the hearts of calloused men,

But of all the works of the Master's art,

The greatest to me is a caring heart!

QoS

Touching Latvia

Photographing a "Touching Latvia" music team,

I saw onrushing crowds pause, mesmerized,

Their stoicism warmed by singers from a far land,

As they eagerly received flyers on the "Savior" concert.

A little girl's ponytail bobbed and swirled

As she joyously danced to the music of the Savior's love.

A bearded man dropped on to the bench beside me,

Seeking to express his appreciation in Latvian.

Oh, East is East, and West is West,

But contrary to Kipling's epic poem,

The twain did meet on the streets of Riga

Through God's universal gift of music!

eless +
ungry

MERRY
Christmas!

THE FIRST
Christmas

Prophets of old through God foretold:

"The virgin shall conceive a child,

And he shall be called Emmanuel…"

As shepherds guarding their flocks by night

Heard angels and saw a great light,

And wise men from their lands afar

Were led to Christ by His wondrous star,

The Savior born on a bed of hay

Brings light and love to our day,

Giving new life to all reborn

Thru the RISEN SON of Christmas morn!

Joy IN HEAVEN

Shepherds heard joy in heaven above

On the first Christmas long ago

As God sent the greatest gift of love

That you and I could ever know!

Two millenia have passed away

But Jesus still calls us today

To follow the wondrous light

That gleamed on the first Christmas night!

Christmas at the *Grandfolks'*

This time of year, our minds return
To an evening long ago:
The shining tree that seemed so tall
To wondering eyes below,
As Christmas at our Grandfolks' house
Set every heart aglow.

As we celebrate the season
With gifts and ornaments fair,
May the true spirit of Christmas
Fill our minds with love and care,
Until the miracle of Bethlehem
With all the world we share.

A baby in a manger born
Was seen by few on Christmas morn,
But rising from that bed of hay,
His power extends to our day,
Bringing new life to all reborn
Thru the RISEN SON of Christmas morn!

Christmas

With Roman power at its peak

God's people knew a future bleak,

So a baby in a manger born

Was seen by few on Christmas morn.

But reaching from that bed of hay,

His pow'r transcends this fearful day

To save the souls of all reborn

Thru the Risen Son of Christmas morn.

On the starry night
Of Jesus' birth
The angels sang
Of peace on earth.

Now war and hate
Beset our day,
And joy and peace
Seem far away.

But His Word rings
Across the years,
Transcending all
Our doubts and fears.

True peace belongs
To those who pray
To the Risen Son
Of Christmas Day!

Glory to God
IN THE HIGHEST

On the first wondrous Christmas Day,

Humble shepherds heard angels sing

Of Jesus Christ the newborn King:

If we humble our hearts and pray,

Could we, too, hear the angels sing

And every day be Christmas Day?

OQS

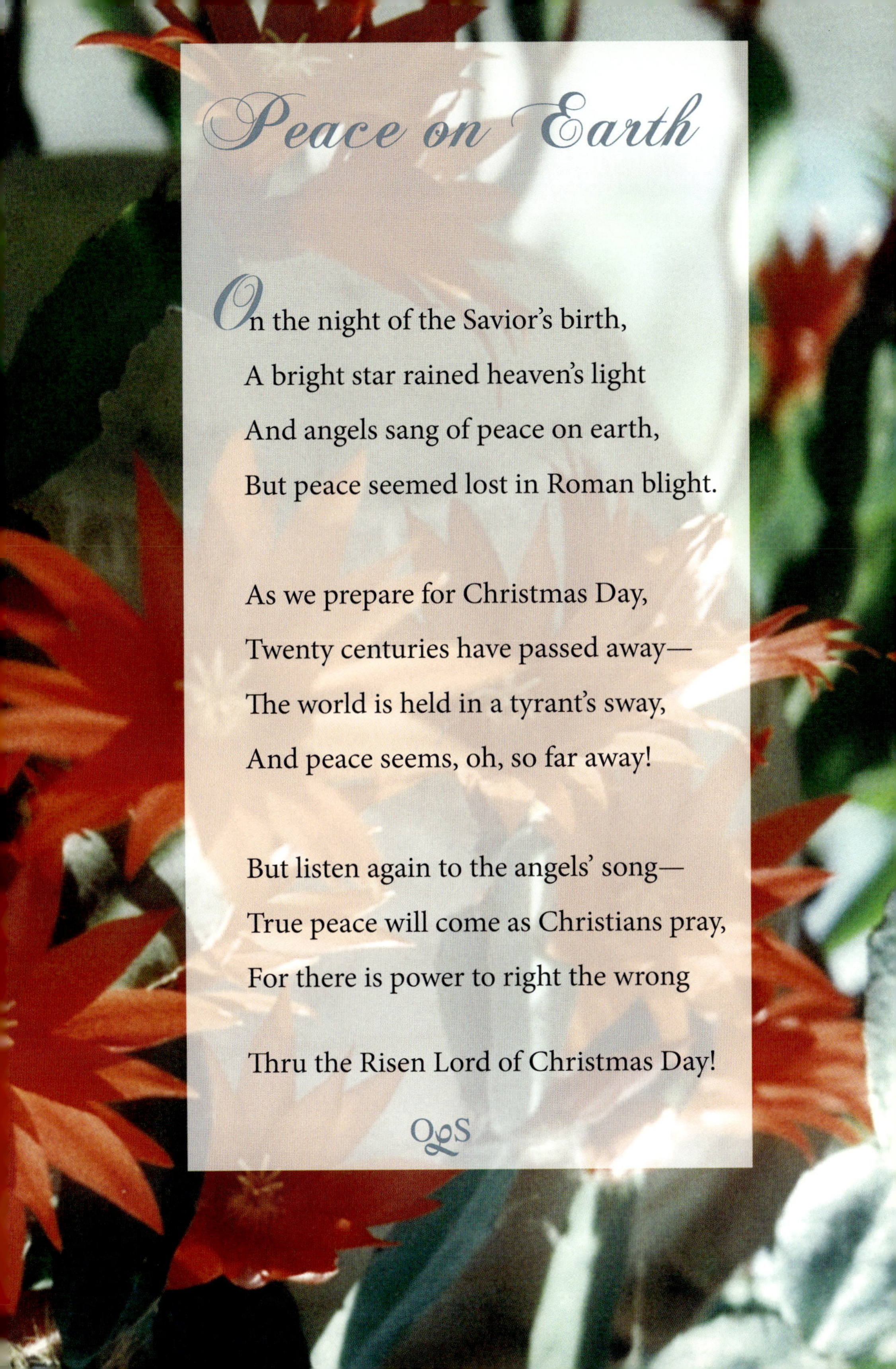

Peace on Earth

On the night of the Savior's birth,

A bright star rained heaven's light

And angels sang of peace on earth,

But peace seemed lost in Roman blight.

As we prepare for Christmas Day,

Twenty centuries have passed away—

The world is held in a tyrant's sway,

And peace seems, oh, so far away!

But listen again to the angels' song—

True peace will come as Christians pray,

For there is power to right the wrong

Thru the Risen Lord of Christmas Day!

QᴏS

To My Wife

The trails we tread together,

All abloom with flowers fair,

Remind me of the blessings

I'm privileged to share.

The trials we bear together

In a dark, fearful hour

Help us to depend on the

Presence of His power.

The seeds we plant together

In the SONshine of His smile

Yield living fruit eternal

To make our lives worthwhile.

The home we make together,

With loving, caring hearts,

Gives me a glimpse of Heaven

Where all true marriage starts.

Happy Anniversary!

You captured my heart

With blossoming grace,

The loveliest rose

In the marketplace.

And the world stood still

As I married you,

That breathless moment

When you said, "I Do."

Though the years have flown

At a dazzling pace,

They've left no sign

On your lovely face.

And I thank the Lord

Each wonderful day

That I walk with you

On the Heavenly way!!

Happy Valentine, Love

At the time when weather hangs in the balance,

Waiting for a pronouncement by the harbingers:

The robins who stop to hop on their way north;

Daffodils bravely pushing up golden antennae;

Trees rushing the season with new green cloaks

In the face of yet-cold winds, rain and snow—

The world waits breathlessly in eager anticipation

Of something beyond human imagination—

Miraculous new life, bursting out in all its glory

To honor the Creator and bless His children.

It's time to celebrate with hearts and flowers

That speak louder than frail words could do

To tell the incomparable love of the Savior

And the eternal love that I have for you!

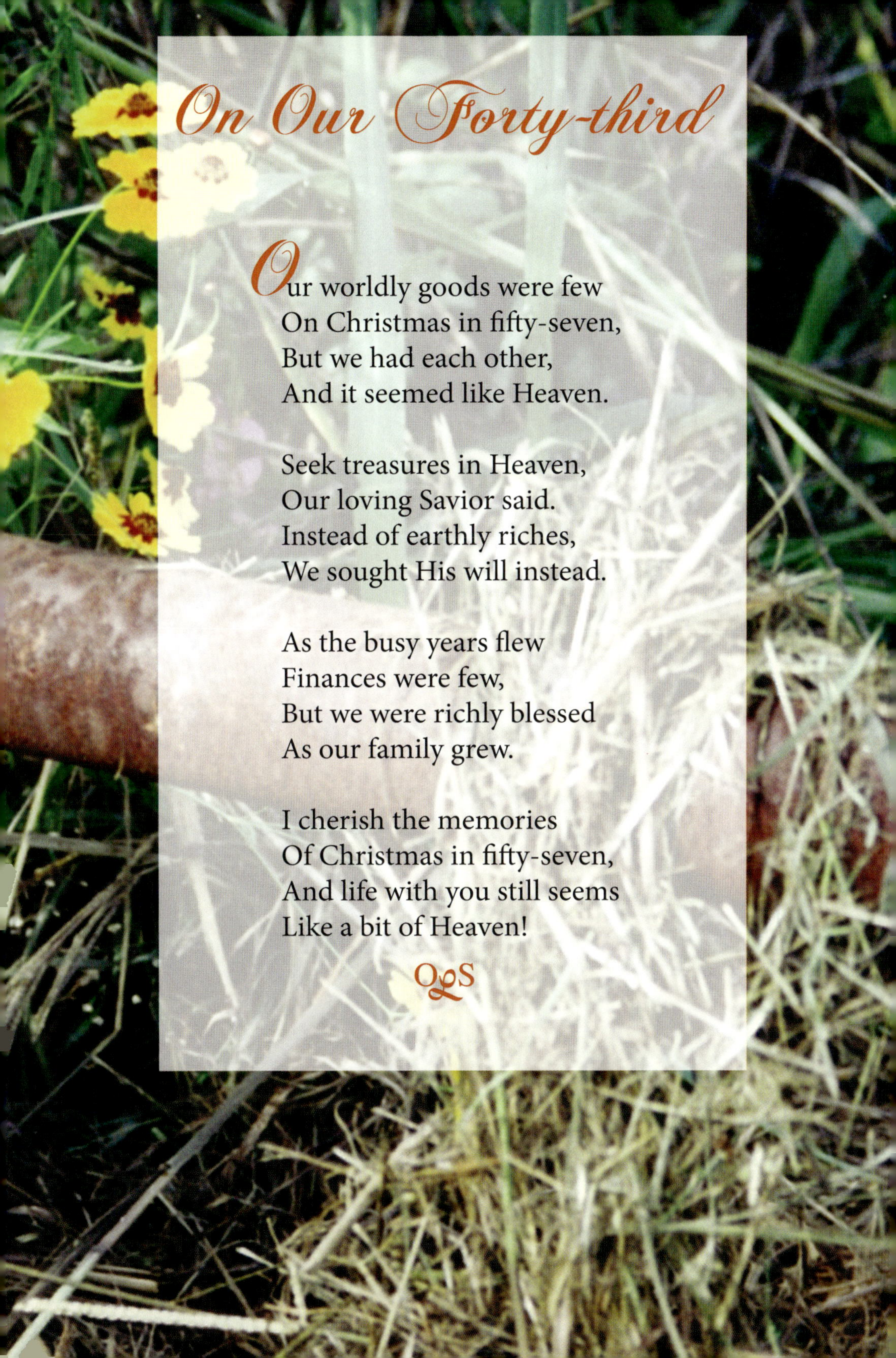

On Our Forty-third

Our worldly goods were few
On Christmas in fifty-seven,
But we had each other,
And it seemed like Heaven.

Seek treasures in Heaven,
Our loving Savior said.
Instead of earthly riches,
We sought His will instead.

As the busy years flew
Finances were few,
But we were richly blessed
As our family grew.

I cherish the memories
Of Christmas in fifty-seven,
And life with you still seems
Like a bit of Heaven!

OLS

TO MY VALENTINE, *1996*

Howling coyotes and creepy, crawly critters

Are surely destined to give you the jitters,

But when chips are down and troubles mount,

You're always the one on whom I can count.

I was drawn to your heart so gentle and kind

And deeply impressed with your inquiring mind;

Your sparkling wit and unquenchable cheer

Bring joy to my life whenever you're near.

Sweet missiles of love on Valentine's Day

I fain would compose to brighten your way,

But the plain simple words I'd like to say:

I love you more with each passing day.

OℓS

To My Love on
Our Fortieth

My love is like a flower fair

Spreading its fragrance in the air.

My love is like a tender song

Soothing my spirit all day long.

My love is like a warm spring day

Driving the winter far away.

My love is like a starlit night

Bathing my life in heavenly light.

My love has made my life so sweet,

I'm glad she swept me off my feet.

Thankful for all that's come before,

I'm looking forward to forty more.

QPS

To My Love on the Eve of a *New Millenium*

When the icy storms of winter

Beat against my window pane,

You're the warm sun of springtime

And the soothing summer rain.

When arrows of disappointment

Pierce the high hopes of my heart,

You're the balm of restoration,

Lifting me to a brand new start.

I'll embrace the new millenium,

With no fear of life's weather,

Because of the wonderful day

God joined our hearts together!

ON OUR
Forty-seventh

When first I saw you in the store,

Your smile like the sun on a spring day

Illumined the crevices of my soul

And gently stole my heart away.

Our first date was certainly blind:

You thought I came to visit Jay,

But I stayed and went to church

With your folks that fateful day.

Many years have come and gone

Since that wondrous unique start

As my love I pledge anew

And thank the Lord with all my heart!

HAPPY BIRTHDAY, *Darling*

On good days and bad,

In glad times and sad,

You're the sweet sunlight

That follows the night.

I thank God above

For His matchless love

And wonderful life

With you as my wife.

Wherever I go,

Whatever I do,

It'll be in the glow

Of my love for you!

To My Darling
with Love, 2007

As I look back across the years

Of indescribable joys and tears,

There were many who blessed my life

And the greatest became my wife.

In Antioch's arbors God prepared

A treasure who lovingly shared

With a lost and dying earth

The News of the Savior's birth.

Vainly I search for the words to share—

Sweetest of the sweet…fairest of the fair…

Fifty years have come and gone:

Often apart, but never alone,

We pulled together through smiles and tears,

And I can't wait for the next 50 years!

EVANGELISM

Unlocking the Silent World

How wonderful is the human ear,
Taken for granted by folks who hear,
But some have never had the choice
To listen to their mother's voice.

In all their life they've never heard
The medley of a mockingbird,
Nor the sigh of a summer breeze,
Whispering softly in the trees.

Imagine if you had never heard,
You wouldn't know how to say a word,
Adrift on an ocean without sound,
With rocks and shoals all around.

But God sent Bob Parrish who understands
And speaks a language with his hands.
Into the silent world he came
Serving and caring in Jesus' name.

The Word of God's grace he unfurled,
And now those living in the silent world,
Can walk in the light of the Risen Son
Till the day they hear Him say, "Well done!"

Like Never Before

Tell His love while there is light,

Very soon will come the night;

He who's worthy of life's best

Will gently lay us down to rest.

With sowing and reaping past,

We shall sleep but wake at last

To greet again in Heaven above

Folks to whom we told His love.

So, let us serve with one accord

In the pow'r of the Risen Lord,

And may this ever be our goal:

"Tell His love to every soul!"

Keep Looking Unto Jesus

I'll keep looking unto Jesus,

Who's the Savior of my soul,

I'll trust His tender mercies,

And His grace that made me whole.

I'll keep looking unto Jesus

Thanking God for all He's done,

And bear His cross with patience

Till my earthly race is run.

I'll keep looking unto Jesus

Who endured such shame for me,

And I'll tell His love to others

Till His face at last I'll see!

Whatever It Takes

Christ, to ransom me from the fall,
Bled and died upon a tree,
Am I willing to give my all
For Him who gave His all for me?

Meekly assuming the servant role
To the lowliest souls I meet,
And like Him who made me whole
E'er be willing to wash their feet?

Am I willing, whatever the cost,
To give my Lord what it will take
To share his Gospel with the lost
And give my all for Jesus' sake?

Whatever it takes, Lord use me up,
As I thirst to do thy pleasure,
Willing to drink from Jesus' cup,
To lead the lost to Heaven's treasure!

OᴗS

His Mind
in Me

Because thy love
From Heav'n above
Came down to earth
Thru Jesus' birth…

Dear Lord I pray,
That, day by day,
The world may see
His mind in me!!

OQS

ONE IS
NEARER
TO
GOD
IN A
GARDEN
THAN ANY
PLACE
ELSE ON
EARTH

A FLOWER

God wanted to plant a flower
In a harsh and barren place,
So he found a warped seedling
Rejected by the human race.

Men said the plant was hopeless,
But He reached down deep inside
Replacing its horrible evil
With His love so deep and wide.

Nurtured by God's gardeners,
It took firm root and bloomed,
Sharing His precious SONlight
With the hurting and the doomed.

The plant that's dry and wilted—
Cast away by human hands—
Can blossom with life anew
In the Master's loving hands!

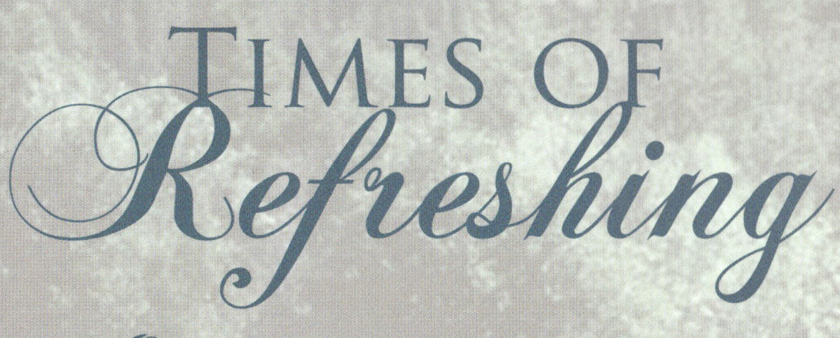

Our Lord who gave all does continually yearn

For hearts grown cold to repent and return

To times of refreshing as in days of old

When disciples were led to a witness bold;

Where holy fires consume sin and strife

And we serve again in abundant life.

Times of refreshing is our souls' fervent plea;

Grant it, oh Lord, to Christians like me

Whose hearts may warm and beat with His love,

Leading sinners to the Savior above!

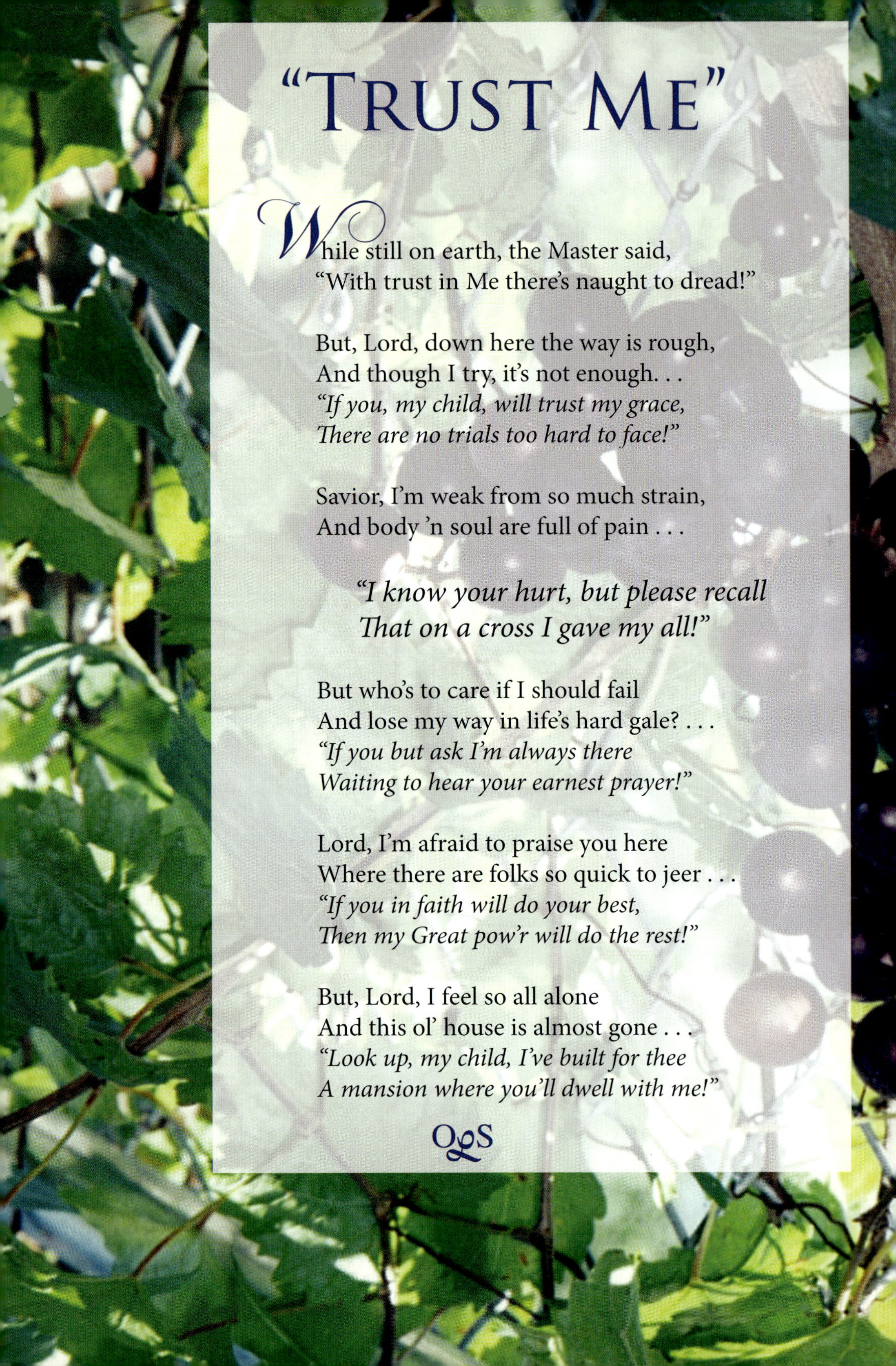

"Trust Me"

While still on earth, the Master said,
"With trust in Me there's naught to dread!"

But, Lord, down here the way is rough,
And though I try, it's not enough. . .
*"If you, my child, will trust my grace,
There are no trials too hard to face!"*

Savior, I'm weak from so much strain,
And body 'n soul are full of pain . . .

*"I know your hurt, but please recall
That on a cross I gave my all!"*

But who's to care if I should fail
And lose my way in life's hard gale? . . .
*"If you but ask I'm always there
Waiting to hear your earnest prayer!"*

Lord, I'm afraid to praise you here
Where there are folks so quick to jeer . . .
*"If you in faith will do your best,
Then my Great pow'r will do the rest!"*

But, Lord, I feel so all alone
And this ol' house is almost gone . . .
*"Look up, my child, I've built for thee
A mansion where you'll dwell with me!"*

QૃS

Where Is Your Heart?

A heart for Jesus the Master sought

And with his blood the ransom bought;

Oh, that we had the Savior's heart

To show sinners a brand new start.

Compassion for people now He seeks,

From crowded slums to snowy peaks;

Oh, won't you have the kind of love

That points the lost to Heav'n above?

Where is your heart, the Master asks;

Is life consumed by worldly tasks,

Or do you find the time to pray

For unsaved souls along the way?

SONLIGHT

May the SONLIGHT of His love

Fill your every precious hour,

Till you shine for God above

Thru the presence of His power.

TEMPTATION

O, the tempter waits each and every day

To lure our souls from the Heavenly way,

But God loved sinners like you and me

And sent His Son, Jesus, to set us free.

No temptation's ever too great to bear.

If we confess it to Him in prayer,

He's waiting to give us His very best

And lead us to pastures of perfect rest!

Look Unto the *Field*

"The harvest is plentiful,
But the laborers are few."
Oh, will you accept
His commission for you?

Jesus is seeking
In you and in me
A love for sinners
He died to set free.

They come in all shades,
But each is our kin;
If we don't win them,
They'll die in their sin!

So lift up your eyes,
Go forth in His shield,
As Christ commands us:
"Look unto the field!"

Earle C. Powell & Son
Enterprises
Carthage, TX
(214) 693-6691

MISCELLANEOUS

THE ANASAZI BEAN

Oh, the ancient Anasazi
Is more than just a bean.
Listen to its history,
And you'll see what I mean.

On the cliffs of Mesa Verde
B'neath the Colorado sky,
God gave it to the Indians
On the plateaus high and dry.

They left amid the ruins
When their ancient culture died,
Some pretty speckled beans
That seemed almost petrified.

Then came another race
Who were astonished to find
The beans were still alive,
Once more to bless mankind.

A Good Place to Eat

I know of a wonderful place
Called Mama's Daughter's Diner.
You can travel around the world
And never find one finer!

There's larrupin' meats and veggies
And pies of scrumptious amount.
But beyond the great home cookin'
It's good folks that really count!

Hymns We Love
IS FORTY

With anthems strong and flags unfurled
For two pioneers in the broadcast world,
We offer this verse as a Christian toast
To *Hymns We Love* and its warm-hearted host.

Whether you're happy or feeling forlorn,
The very best way to start Sunday morn
Is to tune your dial to the sunshine way
And let *Hymns We Love* brighten your day.

Search the world, and I'm sure you'll find
It's the oldest program of its kind;
Born in the heart of Norvell Slater,
It can move the heart of a music hater.

It began in the year of fifty-two
When hymn recording was near brand new,
When Graham and Shea had barely begun
Telling Good News of God's Risen Son.

If we could do hymns the way you do,
We'd create a song deserving of you
To let folks know on its date of birth
There's no greater program on the earth.

In the heavenly quest you stood the test,
As you gave the Master your very best;
So, bask in the joy of a well-earned glow,
For *Hymns We Love* is forty, you know!

Thanksgiving Square

Great were the wonders of the ancient world,

From pyramids to Babylon's gardens fair,

But there are some modern great wonders, too,

Tho none compare with Thanksgiving Square.

God planted a seed in the heart of a man

Who'd dare to dream an impossible dream:

A city block 'mid the traffic din

With trees, grass and a flowing stream.

It beckons the weary to rest awhile

As melodic bells peal to their souls

And lift them above the maddening pace,

Reminding them of higher goals.

At the heart of it all is a symbol divine,

A chapel where folks stop and share

Their reverence and gratitude

In the world's only Thanksgiving Square.

The Beekeeper

O, the beekeeper is a fearless man

Who's fed mankind since time began—

His eyes overflow with smoky tears,

His face is marked by the stings of years.

He lives his life 'mid flowers and woods,

Never blessed with worldly goods,

But he's kept his family sweetly fed,

Following where the bee trail led.

His journey leads though den and dale,

As smoke billows around his veil.

He loves the Lord and serves Him well

Ready to answer the heavenly bell.

GRANDS

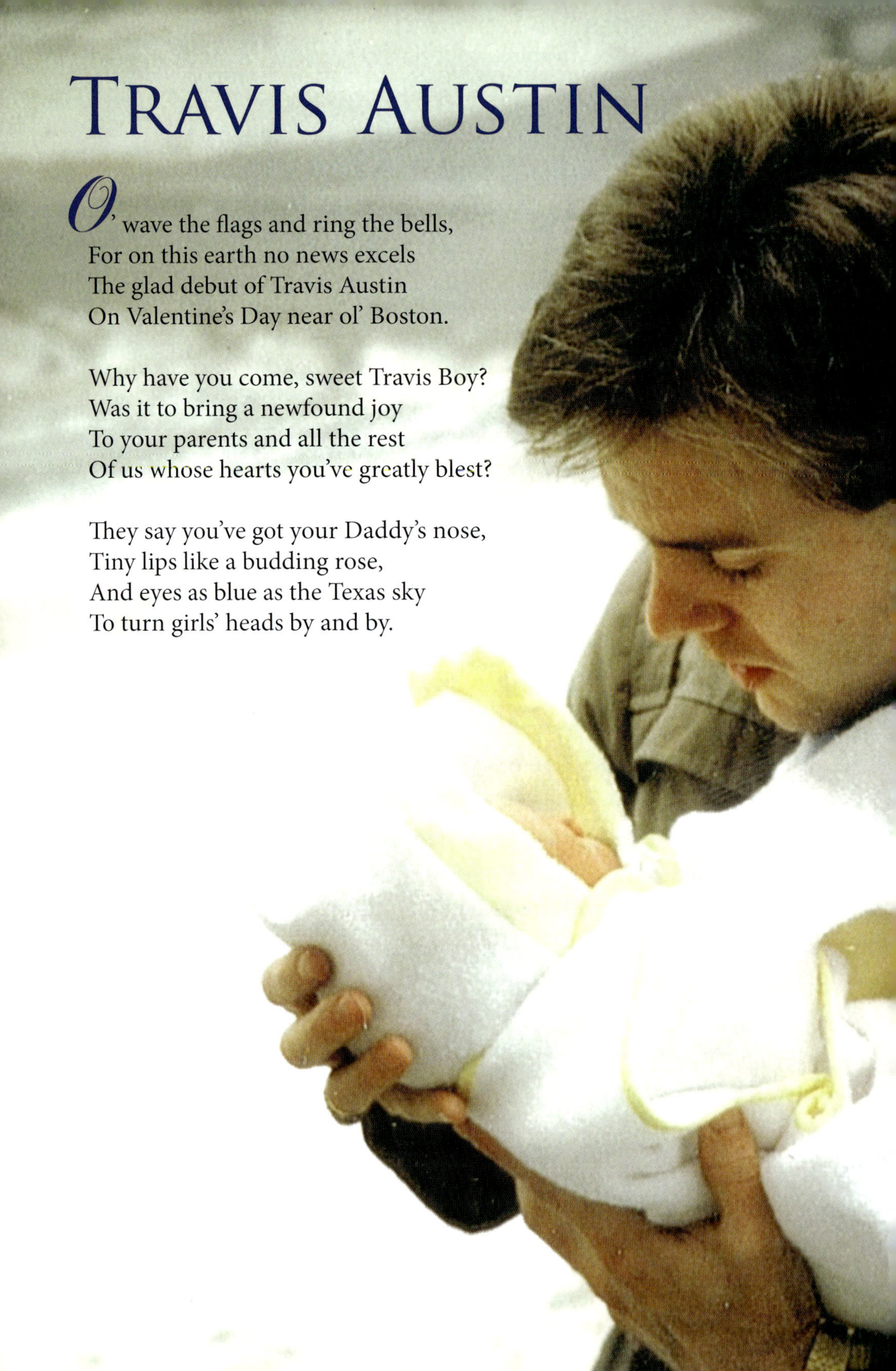

TRAVIS AUSTIN

O, wave the flags and ring the bells,
For on this earth no news excels
The glad debut of Travis Austin
On Valentine's Day near ol' Boston.

Why have you come, sweet Travis Boy?
Was it to bring a newfound joy
To your parents and all the rest
Of us whose hearts you've greatly blest?

They say you've got your Daddy's nose,
Tiny lips like a budding rose,
And eyes as blue as the Texas sky
To turn girls' heads by and by.

As we observe you lying there,
Safe in your parents' loving care,
It's hard for us to understand
That all too soon you'll be a man.

You'll trade your blocks for a bat and ball,
Growing strong and brave and tall—
O' will you reach out for the stars
And be the first to walk on Mars?

Be quick to rise above the strife
And show the world a noble life,
Daring to stand when all seems lost,
To right the wrong, what'ere the cost.

You're the image of God above—
Sweet symbol of the Savior's love—
And in your infant hands and mind
Resides the pow'r to change mankind.

But now inspire us with your charms,
While cuddled in your mother's arms,
And bless us all, wee Travis Man.
You're the greatest since time began!

OℒS

Rebekah Lindsay

A wondrous ray of sunlight
Shone upon the world today,
A precious, living sunbeam
To illumine all our way.

God made her in His image,
With angelic love divine,
And sent her here from Heaven
To brighten your life and mine.

Now she rests in the circle
Of her family's tender care,
Wrapped up in the blanket
Of the love she will share.

Don't blame us if we wonder—
Awestruck with admiration—
If she someday will become,
The leader of our nation!

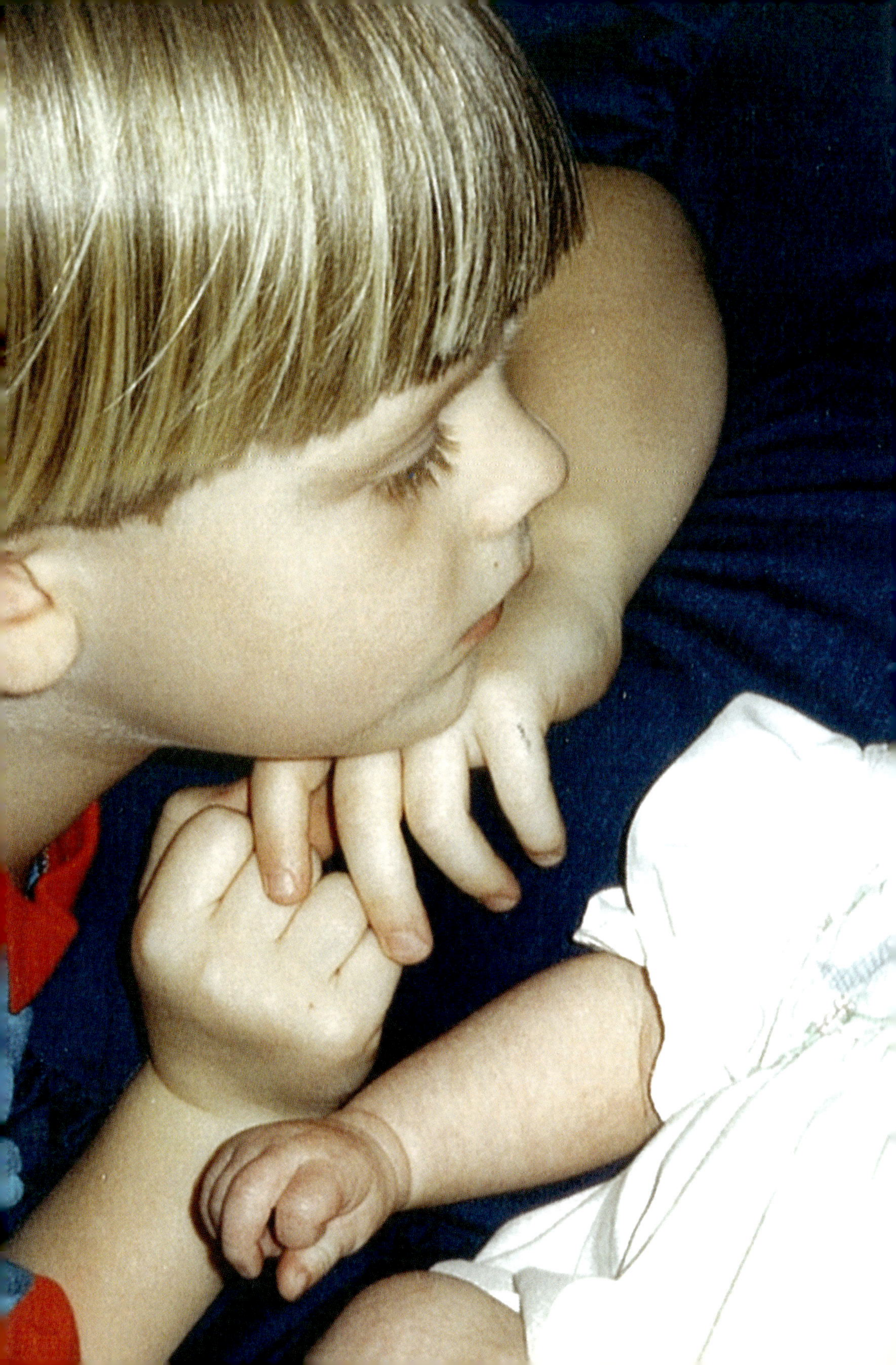

Happy Birthday, Rachel

Here's a riddle for you and me:
Who has a sister named Emily?
Who cheers for Pooh and Tigger, too,
And turns gray skies to sunny blue?
I'll give you a hint: I am told
Our guest of honor's four years old!

Yes, she may climb the mountains tall,
Be a champion in softball,
And one fine day lead our land,
But now the world must understand
This glad news we can't withhold:
Rachel Lee Scott is four years old!!

QgS

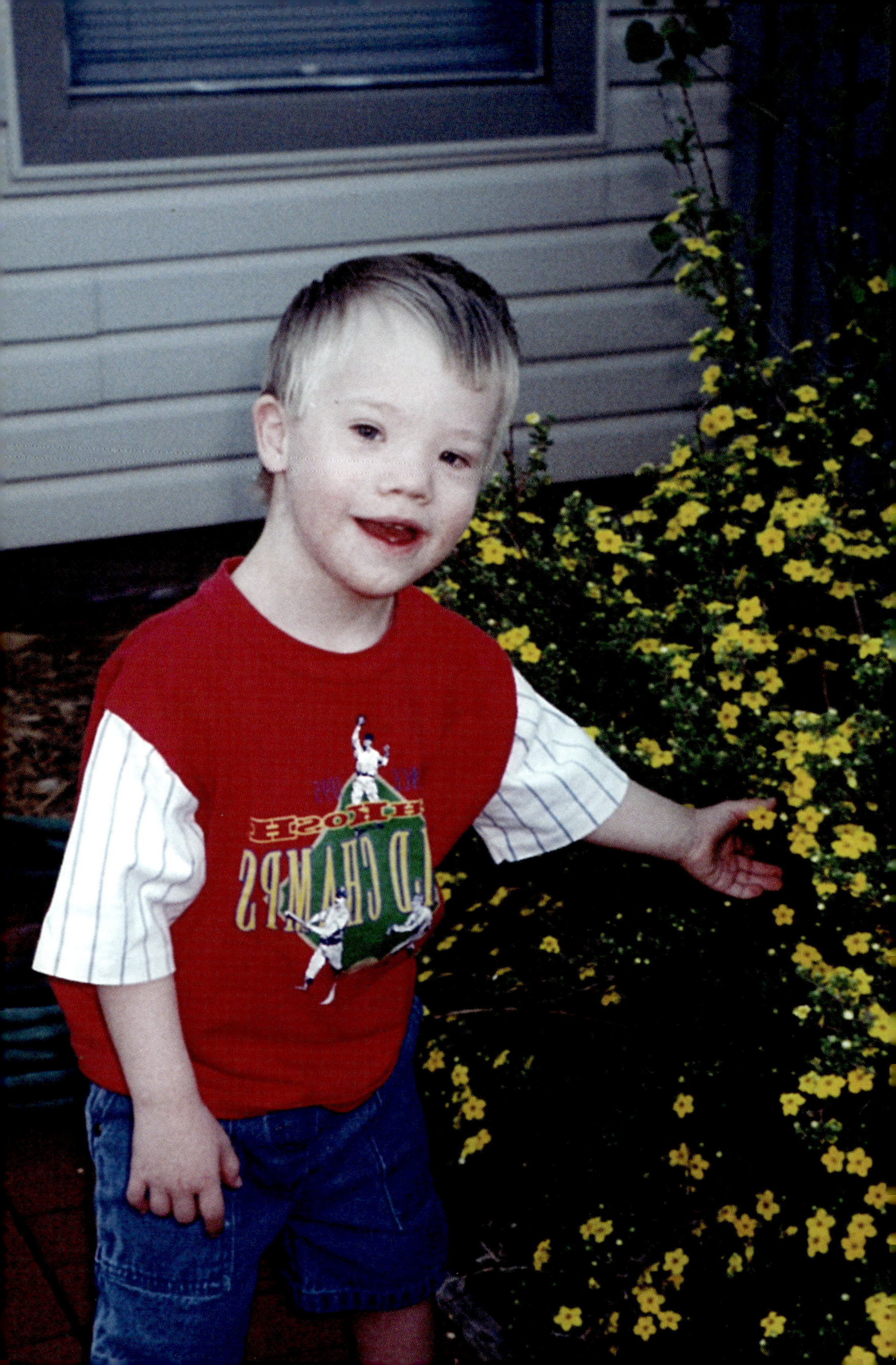

To Michael, Who's Three

God sent a precious sunbeam

In His wondrous, perfect love,

A miracle of His glory

To fill our lives with love.

You've made our lives much fuller

With a taste of the Savior's love,

And we praise Him for sending

Such joy from Heaven above!

Did you know there'll never be

Anyone else like Emily?

She's the one you cannot see

When she hides from you and me.

Beautiful pictures she makes

And tasty, delicious cakes,

And you know what else she'll do?

She'll pick berries and plums, too.

If you ask her she'll confess

She has a true friend named Ches.

Birds and bunnies are her pals

But they scatter when Ches howls.

She spreads sunshine as she plays

And paints rainbows in our days.

There's just one more thing to say"

Emily is four today!

God Speaks

Across the pages of time

In divine prose and rhyme,

God speaks to our hearts

Through His Spirit sublime.

TO THE
Pastor's Wife

Above the cries of her ailing child
And other calls of daily life,
She listens for the quiet voice
Calling her as a pastor's wife.

Her worth is far above jewels,
It says in His changeless Word.
Above the strife and tumult
Her calm, caring voice is heard.

"She extends her hand to the poor,"
And her home's full 'round the clock,
As teen-agers to keen-agers
All make it their place to dock.

With grace not taught in charm school
She shows the sisters and brothers
How the Holy Spirit shining thru
Awakens His love in others.

She sees the souls she counseled
For many a gloomy night
Exchange their sin and depression
For Christ's salvation and light.

Among the lessons she's learned
While doing her chosen task:
Are Christians, too, can have fun
And even take off the mask.

In the throes of her adarkest hour,
When she cries, "God, where are you?"
He whispers in matchless love,

"I am here, child, carrying you."

She's thankful she met a man
Who follows the Lord's command,
And she's happy they can serve
In joy or grief in any land.

She suffers the pain of parting
Each time they answer "the call,"
But the joy in new-found friends
Makes her feel it's worth it all.

She thanks God for letting her
Be all she was meant to be,
Not because she's a pastor's wife,
But because Christ set her free.

DAVID CLANTON

Open the Door

I wandered down a lonely road
Carrying a load of guilt and sin
And from somewhere a soft voice said,
"Open the door and let me in."

I fought the battle all alone
But then I heard the Savior say,
"I won the battle long ago
On a cross on the Calvary way."

Through the fog his voice broke through:
Your broken spirit I can heal
And wash away your pain and guilt
In exchange for a life that's real.

After so many wasted years,
I gave all to the Savior's love
I know when life would close,
I'll dwell with Him in Heaven above.

He sought me out from Heaven above
And paid my sin with redeeming love,
And now I sing a Heavenly song
How He purged my soul with redeeming love.

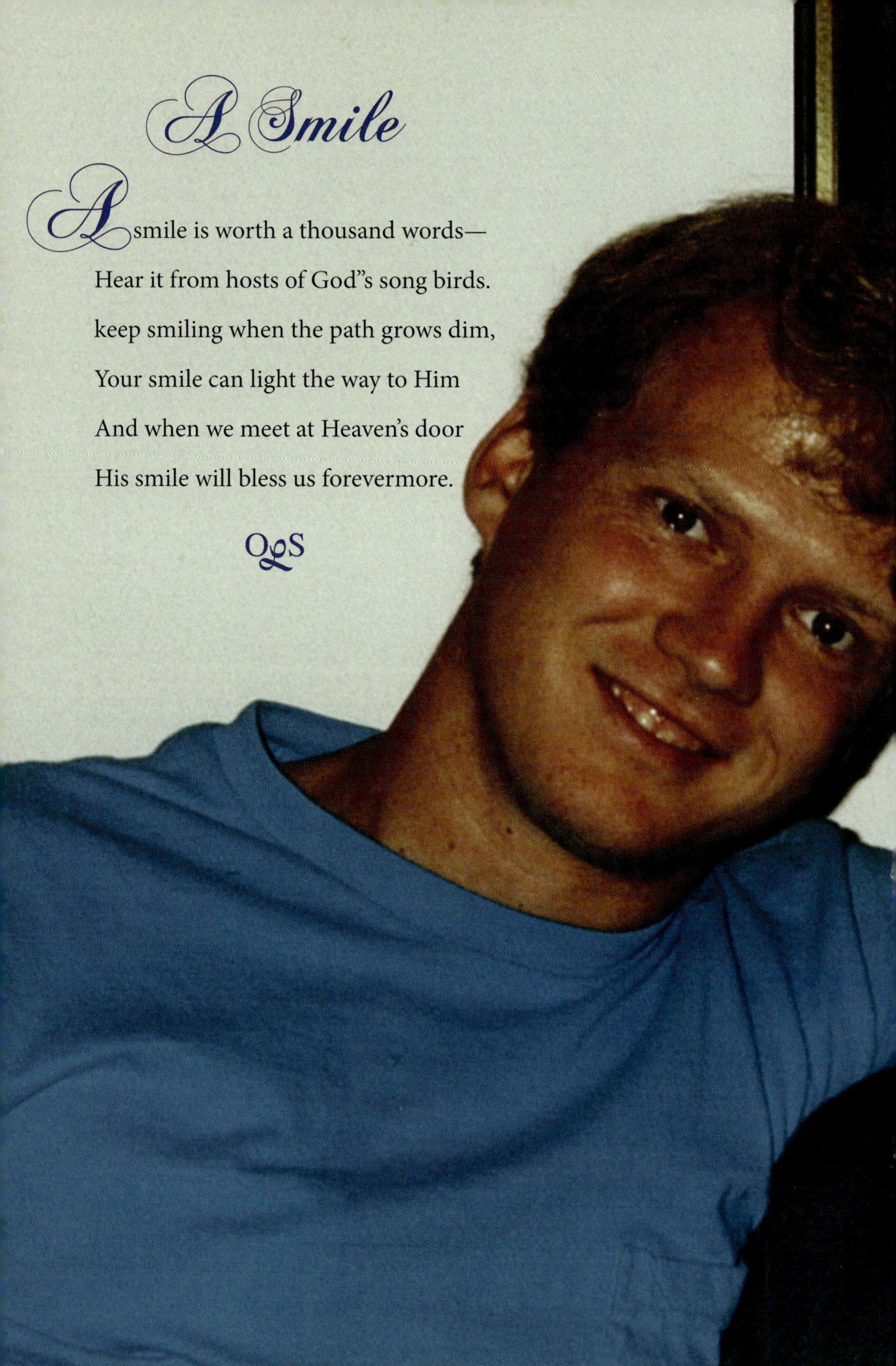

A Smile

A smile is worth a thousand words—

Hear it from hosts of God"s song birds.

keep smiling when the path grows dim,

Your smile can light the way to Him

And when we meet at Heaven's door

His smile will bless us forevermore.

QợS

Snow, 2011

We're a winter wonderland,

Blessed by the Father's smile

With five inches of snow

And time to rest a while.

Along our country road

A single pickup truck

Breaks the solitude.

We wish him good luck.

In the dogwood tree

Cardinals bright red

Forage for food

Hoping to be fed.

There's something we know

'bout our Lord and the snow.

He blesses folks who seek Him,

And His plants bloom and grow!

DAVID CLANTON

Who?

When troubles come like falling rain,

Who stands beside to ease the pain?

When I've no longer strength to stand,

Who steadies me with her loving hand?

When I'm adrift in a sea of despair,

Who lifts me up with a voice of care?

When life's rainbows grow hard to see,

Who clears the fog so tenderly?

When time on earth shall be no more,

Who'll walk with me through Heaven's door?

(Written May 12, 1985)

WHIMSICAL

Ode to East Texas

'Mid the bustling crowd and traffic's roar

Dreams of a homesick country boy soar

To the peaceful scenes of days gone by

Where the tall pines reach up to the sky!

Where dogwood blossoms among the trees

And fields abound in purple-hull peas,

There's fellowship grand and 'tater pie

Where the tall pines reach up to the sky!

I'm tired of the city's maddening pace;

So, set the table and save me a place,

For I'm gonna be there by and by,

Where the tall pines reach up to the sky!

On Seeing My First Emu

By Sparky

(Weisz's pony)

What's this in my pasture now?

It's not a horse or sheep or cow,

It doesn't moo, whinny or growl,

And it doesn't resemble hawk or owl.

I've never, ever been a quitter,

But I'm flabbergasted by this critter.

QS

The Little *Maverick*

Extending the grandchildren's "Secret Trail" through the winter woods to take in the mirror-like beaver pond which temporarily catches the overflow from our lake just before it flows into the neighbors' new lake, I heard the loud lowing of cows across the fence.

Obviously it was feeding time, but the herd faced a major obstacle. They were on the wrong side of the new lake which stretches for about a quarter of a mile to a big earthen levee.

Suddenly a herd leader waded into the cold water and moved gingerly toward the opposite shore while the rest of the cows watched. The water kept getting deeper until it was up to her flanks, but eventually, she emerged from the water and scrambled up the hill on the other side.

Others began to follow her example. One was a cow with a young calf.

"No big hurdle for a grown cow, but what about the calf?" I pondered. "Can he swim?"

Following his Mama trustingly into the icy water, the calf soon was lifting his head high as the water grew deeper and deeper. I automatically held my breath for the little feller as he reached the deepest part of the crossing, but he stood on his hind feet briefly, lunged bravely toward the shallows and, in a moment, was safe on dry land.

The herd leader left the sanctuary of the far shore and came back to encourage those who seemed fearful and hesitant.

I could imagine her saying, "Let's go, you all. It's not too deep."

The herd bull was grazing on fresh green grass on a small island, but he, too, started wading toward the bulk of his herd on the opposite shore. Soon, only one cow and three calves were left on the other side of the lake.

The cow had a good reason for delaying. Her calf was having lunch, as she kept shaking her head to warn to other calves against trying to shoplift a free meal amid the confusion.

As their mothers on the far shore lowed vociferously for them to "come on," the remaining calves were becoming desperate. One of the calves was a maverick who had wandered down the lake from the rest as he questioned the herd mentality, hesitating to challenge the cold water.

I could almost hear him saying, "There must be a better way."

Every time he started to step in, he backed away and drifted further toward the levee. He was now facing deeper water, but isolated as he was, he seemed to take his courage in his hooves and plunged in, only to realize quickly that it was over his head. I breathed a sigh of relief as he re-evaluated the situation, turned and scrambled out.

With sudden determination he took off in a trot toward the levee which he couldn't yet see because it was behind the hill. Soon, he disappeared over the hill, and I waited anxiously for him to re-emerge on the levee.

Surely enough, in a few minutes, far down the lake, a tiny four-legged form appeared on the levee, making good time. As he left the levee, he increased his pace and was welcomed by the lowing herd.

As he arrived into the security of the herd, one of his playmates rushed over to greet him, maybe saying, "What were you thinking?"

"One of these days, I'll be the leader of the herd," the little maverick answered, "and I'll find a way to keep from risking life and limb in icy water."

AUTUMN AT THE LAKE
AND OTHER POEMS
BY
ORVILLE
LINDSEY
SCOTT

THIS BOOK IS
DEDICATED TO
MY WIFE, EMMA JEAN,
AND OUR CHILDREN AND
GRANDCHILDREN
WHO CONTINUE TO
SPREAD THE GOOD NEWS
OF CHRIST
TO A
LOST
WORLD.

AUTUMN AT THE LAKE
AND OTHER POEMS
BY
ORVILLE
LINDSEY
SCOTT
DAVID CLANTON